A Dress Full of Holes

KATHY KUENZLE

ISBN: 978-0-557-40227-4

Editor: Mark Fogarty

Covers: Tony Fradkin

WHITE CHICKENS PRESS

PO Box 1691

Rutherford NJ 07070

For additional copies:

www.lulu.com/content/8597353

Table of Contents

This book is dedicated to my mother, Corinne.

Some of these poems first appeared in Anthologist, Ahnoi, caret, i.e., Clerestory, The Rutherford Red Wheelbarrow, The Bitter Oleander, and Lunch.

All Her Beads: Introduction by Mark Fogarty

This collection of poetry is a cause for celebration.

Many of us in the Rutherford area remember Kathy Kuenzle as a brilliant young poet in the late Seventies and early Eighties, a Rutgers University student and then grad publishing in journals like *Lunch, Lyndhurst Literary Magazine* and *Passaic Review* and reading exciting poems at venues like Fairleigh Dickinson University in Rutherford and the Rogers Museum in Paterson.

Hers was an exuberant voice, playing around with poetic conventions, sprung sonnets that didn't rhyme and didn't scan, words banged together with dactyllic nails, long rushing sentences enjambed or more accurately snapped off in the middle like green beans, stanzas started flush right or two lines from the end of a long poem. And then for counterpoint, images that stopped the rushing stanzas (and your heart) and stood alone like diamonds.

Kathy moved to Providence, RI, in 1983 but luckily, as she says, she took her love of words with her. Who wouldn't be inspired in Providence, the place where Ted Berrigan was born and the river is lit up by waterfires? Kathy took a masters degree at Brown and stayed on.

Her more recent work remains of a piece with her early work. It is populated by family and lovers, natural landscapes, religious ponderings, dreams, whales, Ahab and dresses, lots of dresses: a blackdress, a dress full of holes, a red delicious dress. Add it all together, and you get all her beads: all the poetic building blocks that make garments of words detailed by bright imaginings, prayers, and bewilderments.

Those dresses can be used to fill out the poetic forms Kathy wears so easily and well. They are stitched carefully but with plenty of room left for free association, metaphor, and telling images: *In the mornings / when I light cigarettes/ bees bounce off my hands*. And: *Tender stains drink from the water fountain.* And: *You held my heart like a wafer*. And: *When I turned/in my tinkling dress children fell out / like pennies*. Dresses again!

A Dress Full of Holes is not about poverty. Rather, it is about riches, riches of the imagination and of the spirit, and an openness to creation: the holes are where the poetry comes in.

So we have *red delicious dress*, poems with the sweetness of that variety of apple and the sensuousness of living, love poems like the one to Frank O'Hara, an early model for Kathy, in which the Aster Nuts sign is commemorated *somewhere probably Newark / or passaic* (for the historic record, it was Newark), and a little black girl eating Cheese Doodles and producing orange Russian words, and a nice evocation of her creative process in "Confetti," poems made out of oatmeal, ribbons and green tea, why not?

And then there's *blackdress*, for formal and mourning occasions, a beloved mother gone, the busted sonnet of "The Bridge," memories of lovers, and dreams (which, I am firmly convinced, come from the same part of the brain as poems do). Stuff happens, and it is the stuff of great poetry. There is more detailing, more beadwork, more aching images, like *It rains / like her porcelain fingers tapping/ after dinner.*

The final section, *a dress full of holes*, has as its theme thesis, antithesis, catharsis (not synthesis). It combines youthful exuberance with more mature observation and wisdom. It is time to thank her angels, modestly acknowledge her strengths as a person and as a poet, and think about what is yet to come.

Kathy's afterword is a concise essay about her poetics. It nods to Rutherford's patron saint, William Carlos Williams, describes her bafflement with language poets (I share that one), reclaims her love of words, and concludes *It is not just to say it. It is to say it well.*

A Dress Full of Holes is a wonderful book of poetry. You will enjoy it from beginning to end, and you will remember it 25 years from now, just as I remembered images from her early work 25 years ago. You will remember the dresses she wears her poetry on, and all the beads of Kathy Kuenzle's unforgettable images.

A Dress Full of Holes

red delicious dress

CONFETTI

When I made the paper I put in:
oatmeal, ribbons, green tea.

Two things happened and I lost
my hands in the vat: a birthday

did things behind my back (one), and
the beautiful man gave orders (two).

These are good to use: oatmeal
and ribbons. Tea runs

like a girl away and
she gets older.

In my paper I put the memory.
Your piano two keyboards long.

I put in there too: one bare thigh,
wet black lace. I am so sure

we will never meet again.

The paper was put into the shredder
to become small pieces of colored light

I let go from the bridge we fought on.
These then were the orders of the beautiful man:
confetti, some cognac,

babygrandbabygrand.

APRIL AND A LOVE POEM

a marlon brando movie and this
blonde says to him you hang
my moon for me while outside
the whole world is going through
some kind of puberty with trees even
in new Brunswick stan's
coffee shop is bursting
petals and I have this paper
to write i haven't even
started i can't begin
to forgive myself
holy week this week i forgot
palm sunday ash
wednesday too there is just no
breath in papers and tombs i
cannot wholly concentrate on.

instead
i think about you mostly your
thumb planting little slit moons
above all this and that

if i knew you well enough
we would go to new york and with
everyone and all those lights saying don’t walk of course we

walk.

IT HUNG ON THE WALL

My mother is beautiful through
the stained glass window.
When we were all little children
and a swing was a swing
she taught me how to dance
to Sing You Sinners.
She's the most beautiful woman
in the world to me.
My father would putt golfballs
into pilsners.
An egg in his beer always.
Always a par in sight.

She holds the ladder.
He bangs on the wall for beams.

LOVE POEM FOR FRANK O'HARA

on Saturday morning
after the party which started the
night before and which we had all
had a good time at we drove down
route one and i said it was raining
but it wasn't so i said not
really raining just grey
and good enough to pass for
rain and everyone in the car had
hangovers because we had
had such a good time and it was
december the second but more like
fall and a little cold out but
warm in the car and
no one said a word just
the feeling being good
and we passed a truck which said
goldberg appliances and
i sang goldberg goldberg
appli ances appli ances
until someone in the backseat

took my black
hat wouldn't give it back
causing a commotion because i
was not
about to let it pass without so
much as one word from me and
someone said that was to
my credit it being my
hat and all.
somewhere probably newark
or passaic we drove
past a building it
read: everybody
eats aster nuts
in yellow and red on
grey cement i saw
spacesuits and became sad
and happy at the same time
and there was a big
can of nuts
on top of the building
which looked real i said
it reminded me of doctor t. j. eckleburg in the
great gatsby and someone agreed not
having read it and i
pulled my black felt hat over my ears my

bangs went in my eyes and i said i
wished frank o'hara wasn't dead
and we all
all of us
in the car agreed and
were silent and i made someone
put on the windshield wipers
at that precise moment
although as i already explained
it wasn't really raining.

NEAR WATER

If you put your ear on his chest
you would hear the ocean.

A bracken necklace, a bracken necklace.

One sprig of sea flower
so primal, so pretty.

If you put your ear on him,
if your grace and desire are there, present
in that room

of necklace and scent, you can swim.
You can float or swim,

luckier than Ophelia,
luckier than Ophelia's scantest stroke.

TWO DAYS SINCE

two days since ash Wednesday and what
can i say to that pinchy reminder it puts
color in my cheeks. oh mother you never told
me you'd given birth to such a wonder and spring
closing in just fragrantly blue doing what it
does and i
want to have a baby in tennessee sometime maybe ten
years from now to start the decade strongly with a southern
flower on my right hip like yesterday morning some
boy woke me up and my eyes couldn't adjust to the
light at first i played a jerry jeff walker album so he
could hear and sticky liquor i kissed his
neck just once and maybe i'll remember with rain
smoking up the back porch of some sagging
house in what was it banjo oh
yes tennessee or under a drunken
moon his lovely mouth like grey
stuff on my mortal forehead what
can i say
                my father's eyes bluer
than paris at night and katherine

hepburn somewhere behind
my brown ones while she cried
in the rainmaker matches finger
for charmingfinger the legacy he has
pressed into my palm this one who has
no sons and just a money
less daughter
            oh mother you've married
a handsome man but do not
tell my father and you can see
the helium sky and you can see
the helium sky bloom blue.

IN THE LIBRARY

In the library there was something dead
with titles. It looked like a fish
on its side in the children's section
in the dollhouse holding the fish bowl
open as an anemone and breathing
everything comes up Melville if you read him.

Submerge the city under the Atlantic
and you can only find out it was growing
oceans the whole time. Someone sends out

fingers. Someone receives with ears and your hands read a little
to the left of a Mayakovsky poem
and before it is read
there is one little black girl wearing a summer house
of sweat stairs storm and
blacktop lots nobody plays in under
her blouse the Jesus relief says suffer
the children to come unto me; there is one
littleblackgirl eating cheesedoodles her mouth

in the bag orange Russian words it's amazing
she can digest.

In the library there was something dead.
The carved radiators spilled old books.
The real wood swore heavy
banisters and promised barnacles. There was something
in there living too
   like your hands   my fistful of whale
your ears mouth eyes like an
anemone or love but open-faced like that.

ACCELERATION THE FLOWER

Remember that time
I was Swiss German
and you were from the Holy Land,
naked and unruffled
beneath my fingers,
your veins the size of a frog's.
We kissed so slowly
velocity lost his breath.
I made a gift to you of a parasol
fashioned from a Japanese drink,
dipped in the first red
of alarm and lower lips.

Under your watch
I slept on a pillow
softer than an
atom.

In that time we gained
the mute speed of eloquent animals
and an exponential

grace:

sound, centripetal.

LOVE POEM TO AHAB IN BOSTON

Oh I know you; redder than an advertisement
for a japanese steakhouse
in the subway. You suck up blue and large
the night where it grows to match your madness.
the pru and moon a hammock
to hold an inky baby. When it puffs
full you hammer it to a mast.
You call it a doubloon.

***

Why won't you ask me to marry you ahab?
And I could have your children and I could be your dinghy and
they would start to grow and they could be my perfume and
    they
could be your sticky and what would they think of us would
    we be able
to keep them and I could be your lost leg and they would start
    to grow
and you could be my ankle bracelet and what if no one liked
    each other and you

could be their gingersnap and I
could be your whale.

***

Crazed as mace. He leans on cue,
He leans into swells in Kenmore square.
In Kenmore square his swollen canoe.

***

He is greener than kelp at the aquarium. We go there
muted as pigeons and scalloped as drugged sleep.
He is lovelier
than the swanboat of Audrey Hepburn's gloved hand
in everybody's public garden, more inscribed
than the monument to ether you can find there if you go.

***

Brownstones on beacon list.
And you could be my sailor.

***

I hear you in the shower singing.

You want your heart turned inside

out. You carve the soap
a spout. Delirious with water. Obsessed by depth.
I plug it with a pearl.

FROM PROVIDENCE

Seeds planted on the path,
pink Rhode Island roadsides flower.
There was a diner, a wound,
a ribcage doused with love.

You were the diner.

If God prayed a prayer who would he pray to?
In my red delicious dress
I crouch behind the throne
to hear light years
of silence between each uttered missive.

In my infernal dress
that you pull off and on me,
often off,
in this small, small place

this thimble's thimble.

blackdress

OCTOBER

It rains. I wake up with a dead relative
hovering above my face as if my face
were a word. She is beautiful
and my eyes blink on her
humming fiction. It becomes important
for the day. Riding the bus
it is important. Drinking coffee too.
It rains like fingers coming
down on piano keys all day. It rains
like her porcelain fingers tapping
after dinner. It strains against her
dead face. It strains further
against her platinum hair.

PINS

The giant autumn descends,
A large cat on a small road
Parading a black paw.

Your wife is a foreigner,
A mediocre spy.
She overstirs the stew.

I hold a pretty gun to her head.
Both apples and
Leaves fall,

Truculent, viral.

You say you've never loved her,
A fistful of pins between her teeth
For every hem.   I believe you

In the dark lane,
Ridden old couch from which,
Across the deviled moment

We toss innominate voodoo.

NOCTURNA

Blackdress.
If a parchment
swelled up to kiss you
with the puffiness of penny words.
Mustang, go lap
a phrase. Baby, love
on the outside.
If my text could burst: pintos
and planes.
Come play.
You are pintos and planes.
I remember our mouth.
Apache. I am in
a blackdress.

Moon rose.

IN THIS MOMENT

it is snowing in Boston. A candle
is lit for my dead grandmother. I
can't bear these things: the steady fall
of roughened diamonds outside
of me, the old woman pearls around
the carpet removed from me.
Oh god in this
moment of first and early clutter
I would desert a jewel also and lumber
toward you and fall from you.

ANGELUS

She knew large spaces having flown, churches
lit gray like wash hung out in rain. She kneels
and holds the flame to wick, her prayer searches
the constellations candles make. They deal

a dark with star-marked pull. An angel's
hand she holds. The broken clay abrupt and strange
to find at altar's foot, to be so banned,
so shook from arm, winged back, oiled eye. A change

she sees the first fall in: angel, then not.
She knew descent having flown: some wax,
whose wings, a sun. Herself, a spot
in movement on the canvas, downed. She lacks

good words for prayer. She shapes her mouth in ways
she thinks are blooms, are calls, are pinks, are bays.

PARADE

It is the parade of you without me.

Your wife twirls the massive baton,
kicks her leg over the gutters
of the roofs.

All of these years I have spoken only to animals.

Swinging by you do not see me
disguised in their thick sanity,
a brass-filled lick as the color guard unfurls

you, who bring up the rear
and carry the inevitable band.

PANEL ON MENTAL ILLNESS

He has held out his hands.
She is telling that within a year
she will kill herself, "off a high building
or in front of a train". She did
not see his gesture, thinking
of her brothers, gliders,
or a twist of skirt on a rail. His thumbs
curl with unstruck embarrassment.
He does not know what to say.
The camera coasts over
the water tumblers.
The crew too may be stunned,
may have daughters, may live
in high rises. His hands go out
a second time, she has attempted
this more than once.
Now looking down
at the possibility of wind,
her fingers wear gowns; tulle floats
towards his grasp. It is the end
of the talk show. The host
is charged, their grip
focused in on, elevated.

AHAB CONSTELLATES

Since you no cache of meteorites,
No stunning or stung,
Stones are not heavy,
The ocean shifts in my hands.

Cetus since that night the years have colluded
And become billions of years.
My happiness swims in the light years,
A whale lost in white stars,

Its brain full of perfume.
Its perfume lost.

LOVE TO HEAR PERCUSSION

This is the sax
in my future boyfriend's mouth.

Turn the beat around.

I note your engagement
six weeks after that abrupt good-bye.

Quando, quando, quando, quando.

His magma swells the fissure
of a mouthpiece. You were not

my greatest love. Now make room for Sammy,

Frank and Dean. In this entropic storm
I pause to take umbrage at your inelegant betrayal.

De bleu, de pinto, de bleu.

Keep your tuba, dirty dog.

Loyalty is the beauty of my lava.

Tiny bubbles. Love
to hear it, love
to hear it.

YOU REMIND ME OF THE OCEAN

(For my mother)

Corridors skin scales trays
corridors wheedling feeding tubes
tubing bodies morphine dripping flowers
visitors veins vases tumblers johnnies cords
pulleys carts tumors the surfacing depths you
remind me of the ocean your diving beauty always
radiation poison nothing can stop stop your beauty
hemostatic anabolic rate centrifugal spin to slow to still things
vital clutched hands tumors tumors drip and panic cells cells
cells and I would kiss the feet of statues and you would eddy
and abate bruises hours gift shop stillness rise and fall and rise
and fall let the moon sleep and wake to its chosen profession as
urine collects and clouds is emptied as specimens multiply mutinous
membranes their collusion flowers. You remind me of the ocean.

There was bravery, always, in the sweet petition of your face,
and bravery tipped its tophat as the ship listed.

PICNIC

It is the old show of holes and bullets.

He says
if he were deserted
on an island with her

he would go look for a horse.
He says she is old, deciphered
trash. He has
bags under his eyes and
a twenty year old wife who laughs

like a pony.
The man sitting across
from him has blue eyes
on two olives. The man sitting

across
is my father.
My father wants to shoot

golf with him a hundred
dollars a stroke in the heat. He says
he doesn't want my father's money. He carries

cash. Thousands on him
daily. He goes to swinging
joints. Then there is something

about pistols and brownstones.
I am not sure what
this is, but I am sure

what this is not.
this is not a picnic.

a dress full of holes

PALE WATERS

You held my heart like a wafer.
I was your sister. We grew as twin
cells. She held all colors
and numbers, our mother.
We swam through the mystery
of liquid coiling holding shape.
So tender, pale and pink, no language
separated us. I could put my finger
in and out of your eye.
You held my heart like a wafer.

LATE BOUQUET

This morning
in the garden
I crouched low
and smelled the both
of us 20 billion years ago
in that superdensity characteristic
of the age. You
were so heavy
as was I
waiting in chaos
for matter's spread
and space
about to be born.
You looked like honey and
God was everywhere and I
saw petals prematurely.

When that smallest door opened
for the biggest crowd
I couldn't see you
for the dust,

all particles speeding
in the pull of that
most brilliant plan.
I was a virgin.
You were a cowboy.
There was a promise of verbena in my hair
and the infants time and gravity.
I am still dizzy
remembering when time
was 10tothenegative43 seconds.

This went on for 19 billion years.
I smelled roses, lavender, lilacs, gardenias.
You said they were in my head
and laughed
as you occupied yourself
with startled
shape. Finally last night
you said in the dark
I had always been
the premonition of a flower.
I said, there's words
for you, and there
is your universe.

THE BRIDGE

There was a bridge the length of the kiss between them.
Sad stars when he left.
She turned her face from the sea,
became satin flowers and the odd shape of his absence.

There was a bridge the length of the kiss.
Between them were sad stars.
When he left she turned her face.
The sea became satin flowers and the odd shape, his absence.

There was a bridge.
The length of the kiss between them spanned a star.
She turned when he left into sad flowers.
Everything was violet then.

Everything was soft and bruised: the
night, his absence and its shape.

A MAN IMPREGNATING A WOMAN WITH APPLES

so they can be red together. He thinks
what he is doing is pungent and slow,
burning snake skins in the rain.
His cigarette smokes down
like a man leaning
against a stone
wall in Pisa
And trotting home from work at five the sky
Was doing something terrible. Something
                    American. She
closes her eyes, paradise darkening and
delicious. This man is the only man
there is: tinypinkflower
                    her little hand in his
                              lost lot.

FALL

Twice a year the tissues leftover
from a careless tonsillectomy
infect. Fall and Spring.
Trinkets remain where a
blonde haired friend
has made her move cross
country. In a wicker
basket she did not take
is a plastic pony and the headless
body of a rider. She herself
rode junior steeplechase. Plastic
foreleg, stirrupped feet,
gloved hands holding reins,
riding suit intact, crop
perfect replica.
The neck as point
of rupture.
It calls back Hawthorne's
story told hoarsely on Halloween.
In the mornings
when I light cigarettes
bees bounce off my hands.

YOUR GARDEN

Your garden says its own name:
me, me, me, me, me.

Its blue voice a pail of honey.

We should sit on this sawhorse
formation of certain molecular

structures. I found this in your garden.
Here is where I say your name

in my yellow voice of combs: you.

Here is the surprise of a sculpted man

and mare, burnish of modest light.
He is slow in giving her the scent

of his strength. Here is the smallest stone.

Knowledge like pollen on your fingers.
Ten matters of great

weight, as if your fragrance was always
here, bewildering the garden.

NOAH

I will not tell how the sky behind
Their backs entertained me, or who started
Train around the bar but that it began.

It was mostly this: wood
That must be made to sing
And the picking of ticks
From couple necks. Then

Everything was wed, each thing
Wed when the cloud burst
Pink its impatience.

POEM
(in one dream)

In one dream of the four your body
over the hudson hung
in suspension on two states
with only one word in
common and you were telling me you could not
bear the bridging
                                        of a hardened youth much
longer with a sanded jersey town and you
were telling me in cliff
language how Satan has the name of Jesus
written on his heart like an unspoken
prayer he cannot be rid of while I witnessed
steel forming on your upper
arms and blue windings of colorlessness the
river flowing under the whole muscled
stretch of you and you were telling me
the hanging was too chiseled
under for you to solely
do with no one to support or slip
you into waterchange and I loved
                                                    you beyond speaking in all

four dreams but hardest

in that one. When I
woke up I looked at my
face on the sleeping pillow
and couldn't believe
it was mine and composed
a piece brownflower
like the toughnib
engine of a train and then I went

awfully far away.

THIS INCH REPRESENTS

The distance from this bridge
to this building is the same
as Providence to New Jersey.

The span between bright stars
is space created between him
and me.

Now New York is fingers with jewelry at night.

Boston is cupboards and grandfather clocks.

Where I live now is thumbs in the fog.

In Providence, where I live now, I learn
of loneliness: birds in a train station.
Tender stains drink from the water fountain.

SEASIDE

On this black path of stars I met you
in the month of the large house and
the week of the sea. When I turned
in my tinkling dress children fell out
like pennies. The words were gathered
and wrung in the garden of that
season behind a heavy gate.

On an unearthly path I saw your face
sick with testimony and coins.
Countless, the yellow minnows
swam and stopped as the bridge
corrupted in your hands and scent
sank weighted. Bottomless.

The night we dreamed of windows
red flowers sat at our table
in the dark. The kitchen
was rendered, a ribbon of first light.
In my voice filled with the sorrow

of newborns: birds, nebulae, a burst

of girls; in my voice of deep
welled sadness the name of our lane
bows down to its cups.
The many names of our lane.

The path of stars.
The month of the big house.

JUNE

Bell tolls.
Ocean swells.
Garbage spills.
Rain slicks.
Cardboard splits.
A blossom tree boughs.
Bell tolls.
Your face is changing to fill
its most beautiful shape.
Your face is held by a shining mind.
You can afford anything:
a measured mile,
a dress full of holes,
dumb luck.

FOR MY ANGELS

Who warp a line of light,
Make burst the real photo.

My sister: soft turn to the jet,
Black haired angel in my cup.

Leaves at the bottom,
A fortune the wind whips

Together and rains on.
I have no brothers

Or sisters. Wayward lights
And sorcerers, too many

Whispers and I miss the home
I have no memory of.

Sweet mother, secret father
Forgive me my angels.

My saucer would remain simple

Circle in a circle
If it were up to me.

If it were up to me
What would I give to see you:

Count them.
All my beads.

MY STRENGTH

My strength is slowly walking.

My happiness is walking in a high hat of terns.
An offer is made involving oceans:
rolling, roiling. Accepted.

My faith is a still fist.

My love is running with the muscle might
of stallions. My love is a pier in the fog.
He remembers my thin frock,
my pale knees in summer.
His heart is a black horse wet with rain.

My strength is walking, slowing, walking.

My beauty is a verdict.

My book is The Separation of Moon
and Tide. It is my fear swimming,
flanked, caught by stealth.

A DRESS FULL OF HOLES

My love is two-ton. Somber. Running.
My love has a cherry in the vise of his teeth.

I decant my truth.

My death is a red wind.
My death is a red wing beating on the sash.
My strength is walking on the tightrope of a quill:
slippered, balanced, slowly.

ON WRITING

I graduated with an MA from Brown University in 1987 and decided to break it off with writing altogether. Language was dashing. It had a fast car and eyes the color of recklessness. There was no stability. No cottage of shutters and red flowers where I would not think too much. I didn't want to think too much. I needed a solid chore with a tangible outcome. I held hands with Science. There were laws, there was a method, there was proof.

There were also words: chiasmata, ganglion, nebulae. I tried not to notice. I tried hard. Four years of pre-med, two courses short of vet school I started to dream poems. Sleeping, I held words in my hands tilting them so light played in the crevices of R's and A's. Pulsar. Reticular. On a cold morning before a physics class, language showed up like a first love, long-lost, on the eve of an elaborately planned wedding. It leaned against a brick wall smoking a cigarette. It showed up like a bad penny.

*

Why did the ram jump off the cliff? He didn't see the ewe turn. This was the biggest education in writing I ever got: the beauty of malleable language. You can put your finger in and out of its eye.

*

So much depends upon a red wheelbarrow glazed with rain water beside the white chickens. I am transformed by this. I am in junior high. I am invisibly plumbed. I want the poet's name in my locket. Later I find that we are from the same New Jersey town. He is dead but I sit on his lawn. A shingle still hangs: W.C.W., MD.

No ideas but in things was tattooed on my forearm as I began to write. I learned that energy was important, and ordinariness. I believed that poetry was meant to mean. One spring when I was about to graduate from college, I found Williams' grave. Two ladybugs were mating on his stone in the sun.

*

Brown was an ocean of language poets. I did not get what my colleagues there were doing. I don't get it, I said. They said feel the texture. I felt the texture. To me it felt like big deal. I felt the texture a few more times. I could not make it mean. This kind of writing will go nowhere, I told myself.

*

What do you call it when all the planets line up?

A string of pearls.

Now that's a metaphor for you, and a reason to be here.

*

Last week I opened up a book: The Best American Poetry, 2002. Crouched in its contents, having a last laugh, were two teachers and two students from my small class at Brown. Just goes to show what I know.

*

It is not to say it. It is to say it well.

www.ingramcontent.com/pod-product-compliance
Ingram Content Group UK Ltd.
Pitfield, Milton Keynes, MK11 3LW, UK
UKHW020234250726
13967UKWH00001B/367

9 780557 402274